ESTEBAN GARDENS

The Spiritual Side of Gardening as Recorded by A Layman's Hand

BY ANNETTE BROCHIER JOHNSON

WITH ILLUSTRATIONS

BY LEAH JAY

FrogHavenLady Series

DEDICATION
For Alfie and My Rogue

With much love and affection,
The Frog

Time to go to print...

...another day's work has finally ended; the clock permits me to stop and call it a day. I used to arrive home with a paycheck in my pocket; today, my answers to prayer are what make the hearth seem even warmer than before; perhaps it will be a popcorn night? A few moments of reverie in the garden before starting dinner are allowed this evening; even the knockout roses are still blooming to full capacity! There is not an empty branch in sight.

I'm beginning to understand my father's tendency to settle for what he repeatedly described as good enough. It has taken me years to believe that an inner sense of peace can be mine more often; I need only see and hear with a grateful heart. There are gifts of solace and joy when life is good enough!

aJb

Copyright © 2012 by FrogHavenLady.com
First Edition. All Rights Reserved.
Bluebird Publishing, St. Louis, Missouri
Printed in the United States of America

Winter

MEET ME AT THE FENCE

I'VE NOTHING NEW TO BROOD ABOUT; ADMITTEDLY I
THINK TOO MUCH.

IT MAY SIMPLY BE ANXIETY THAT BUILDS
A WEIGHT WITHIN.

YES, I TOO OFTEN WANDER OFF, CONSUMED WITH
PETTY STUFF AND SUCH;

BUT THAT'S WHAT IT OFTEN TAKES
TO AWAKEN ME TO HIM.

ON DAYS MY EYES ARE BLURRY, WHEN I'M DECEIVED
BY ONE LESS SENSE,

I CATCH THE BLOSSOMS' SCENT WAFTING THROUGH
MY KITCHEN DOOR:

DRAWING ME OUTSIDE MYSELF –
CHILD... MEET ME AT THE FENCE!

SOFTLY REASSURING ME –
I AM LISTENING... TELL ME MORE...

Seeing Through the Frost

So, I walk within my garden; it is cold; and I am chilled!

I've still earth, but seek a memory of the birds' last summer trill.

I've an old tree standing there. Will I once more see it leaf?

The surrounding ground seems spent; I am filled with winter's grief.

I suppose should I just wander past, and clean the pathways here,

I could wake one morn to Spring! The sun would melt away my fear.

You have left me but a plot of land. What have I to gain from toil?

It's then I grasp Your guiding words: What I sow will grace the soil!

Frail but Faithful

Will we gather at the table and express our gratitude?

Or will rushing, haste and waste extract what is merely low and crude?

I don't want to work my way through foreign practices or thoughts;

I just want to feel your presence, Father –

I want what most have sought!

I want a sign; a small aside to catch my eye… and then:

I may further my day's journey and believe in YOU again!

There are days I seek to understand Your Will for me; I <u>really</u> do!

Other morns seem distant;

If something is amiss, I forget what I once knew.

The months when all seems lost? Yes, I've had a few too many now;
Or the times when turmoil reeks of pain;
When worries consume my humble brow.
The frost but chills my inner doubt; I can't see through layered ice.
You're asking me to follow you; You've not asked once but twice!

I know better, Lord, than to ignore Your Call…
I've a mind and a willing heart! Help me sort the rice from chaff,
Successfully keep ills and loved ones apart. May those who watch;
My weary stance bequeath anew their hearts and minds,
That Everlasting Life may crown us frail but faithful kinds.

Groundhog Grief

Another February 2nd, I can't explain the depression and the grief that imprint upon my heart an underlying ache; at least, not very succinctly. A friend tells me that I have several good reasons that would give anyone cause to sulk or weep. If she says so, okay.

But I can't stand far enough away to see; my eyes are blinded by the blur surrounding me. In fact, it is one very huge blur. The smaller, individual components are no longer identifiable; nor are yesterday's priorities. Today, it is enough that I recognize the colors around me for what they are: a kaleidoscope of unbelievably deep, jewel tones representing an emotional whirlpool. As in a dream, I can't find my way around or out.

Crying would be great. I know I want to cry but don't ask me to explain why. Just believe me when I tell you I know. Yes, I know. But I can't; and won't. My rules won't let me.

I think I'm crashing, so as I have done after any big crisis, my inner voice is giving me permission to <u>quietly</u> crash. Emphasis is on quietly, which in my rules really means to not draw attention to oneself. Remember, others have far greater mountains to climb...

Thus far, all I can voice is a meek "Help." I hear it repeatedly come from my lips, even in the middle of a simple task..."Help." And when someone within earshot wants to know what I need help with, I can't answer. It is enough consolation that I can still be heard...or will be heard...should I ever need to be heard.

What do I physically need? Nothing; I have the blessings of a warm home within which a pantry and the makings of a great meal are there in easy reach. I have clean clothes, a myriad of colorful pins and scarves from which to choose a rainbow of combinations; I can fake style as well as anyone! I have family and friends who care about me. My health is generally good.

Straighten up! What is wrong with you? Go outside and find something to do. The messages of old still ring out, but the choices are old, too. So, I choose to stay inside, away from brighter sun rays that might uncover my quiet despair beneath a carefully honed smile.

It is better that I adjust my focus solely on good things. I shall begin.

I begin by methodically reminding myself that loved ones are on the mend; that good friends are seeking treatment and under care; and, while I've not a song in my heart yet again, the melody will eventually return to draft an entirely new chorus of praise and gratitude for His gifts. Remembering what a good person is supposed to do when facing any veil of tears, I put myself on autopilot.

I smile. I joke. I laugh and see the irony in the mundane. I am grateful for lots of things; especially today, I am grateful I am not a groundhog, surrounded by funny old men in top hats and tails, disturbing my real quest for another beginning, another spring...

Valentine Mirth

For innocents awake to Friendship's arms
Hearts are not just for February days
They are a bit of make-believe
To soothe winter's uncaring ways

A bit of mulch, clay pots, will toy
Violets and lavender bouquets scent
To quiet inlets of a gardener's soul
And ease a snowy discontent

Some wayward bulbs may yet instead
Break forth through frozen ground
Bare branches stretching out their souls
Refuse to hide! Small buds abound

The spring will once again infuse
The garden's air with sentiment
So hearts 'mid greens again amuse
Worn, loving hands only slightly bent

Spring

$18.00 Worth

Having taken the opportunity to visit one of America's premier garden shows, I paid $18.00 a ticket; still ticket shocked, I walked through the gate inside the Cow Palace with really great expectations of viewing exceptional plantings and ground coverings, hopefully some that I might duplicate in my own garden on Esteban.

Unfortunately, I believe the focus this particular year was on little watering and conservative, low maintenance gardening. So, if you can picture a bunch of weed-like, cactus-like, native-like things growing out of the ground, you can picture accurately enough a good many of the display gardens to view. If these postage-size patio spaces are indeed indicative of living spaces, where was Life's Breath with or without smoking? Patio living was now a one-chair space for the Me Generation; hiding places with recirculated water...Gone were any gardens welcoming family and neighbors' kids into the backyard for a barbeque, cold drink, or playtime. These were gardens to view from outside the property line.

So, I'm going back to my trusty, well-worn garden books and the yearly visit to the summer fair grounds should I want to review "new" ideas in gardens for God's living creatures. It's cheaper to play worm digging in my own soil, and infinitely more gratifying sharing the beauty and the house wine with those who wish to linger here.

POPPIES 'GAINST THE FENCE

A MORNING NOT UNLIKE BEFORE; EXCEPT, THAT MARCH DAY, I CHOSE TO SIT

AND IN THE SUN CLOTHE SOUL AND MIND AMID THE WARMTH BEFORE IT QUIT.

MY CHILD WAS SAFE IN SCHOOL THAT DAY, HER FATHER HAVING LEFT FOR WORK;

SO FEW QUIET MOMENTS CAME THOSE YEARS WHEREIN I ENJOYED A WELCOME QUIRK.

FROM TIME TO TIME, I GLANCED TO SEE THE SEEDS I'D SOWN BEFORE THE SPRING.

NOW, POPPIES 'GAINST THE FENCE DID BLOOM; THEIR GREY-GREEN LEAVES HELD BRIGHT ORANGE BLING!

RETURNING TO MY BOOK, I REREAD A LINE OR TWO, BUT GROWING SATISFACTION BROUGHT ME 'ROUND

BACK TO THE POPPIES' BRILLIANT HUE! AH...MY EYES DRANK IN EACH COLORED MOUND.

THE NEWS WAS BRIEF; ENOUGH TO BREAK MY SOLITARY, PEACE-FILLED MORN.

OUR PRESIDENT HAD BEEN SHOT. AGAIN, A SORDID MIND OUR COUNTRY TORN.

MORE DETAILS CAME TO FURTHER INVADE MY PEACEFUL PLACE; IN SECONDS, MY REPOSE FLED.

INSTEAD, THE POPPIES 'GAINST THE FENCE FORETOLD TO ME A POIGNANT DREAD.

I BLINKED BACK TEARS...PLEASE, PLEASE LET ME HOLD THE MORNING'S WARMTH STILL CROSS MY FEET!

BENEATH MY CHAIR THE SOAKED-IN SUN RELEASED ITS EBBING, REMNANT HEAT.

SEASONS PASSED. OUR LEADER LIVED. THE COLD WAR ENDED IN MERE PEACEFUL PRETENSE.

MY DAUGHTER GROWN, I'D MOVED ON TOO. I LEFT THOSE POPPIES 'GAINST THE FENCE.

ANOTHER YARD, A NEW BEDDING PLAN; AGAIN A CHANCE TO SOW AND TILL,

LEAVING HISTORY'S SADDER DAYS BEHIND SO NEW BUDS MIGHT STAVE OFF CURRENT ILLS.

TODAY, I SEEK COMFORTING BLING. MY HEART CRIES FOR ITS FAMILIAR SENSE!

ELUSIVE? STILL BUT, NOW AND THEN, REPOSE RETURNS FROM SEEDED POPPIES 'GAINST THE FENCE.

    2011 – 100TH ANNIVERSARY YEAR OF REAGAN'S BIRTH.

Planting Azaleas in Full Sun

How often thoughts have been crossing my mind these days - the same thoughts with an underlying current of a common theme: specifically, how difficult and pressure filled all our lives seem to be. How any one of us in any number of given situations are struggling; making ends meet, dealing with family troubles, nursing old hurts, reckoning with illness - the worries are endless. Yet how much of our days' precious hours are spent enforcing our own wills and controls over our very own life's garden; indeed, how many of us are furtively planting azaleas in full sun?

Over the years, I have spent countless hours in my very own life garden; vainly, I used to believe that I could keep the growth healthy and vibrant on my nurturing efforts alone. Sometimes, a simple twist of the tendrils and a particular project might even bend to my directive! More often than not, however, I slowly noticed that my insistent nature was no match for the gentle corrections of His Gloved Hand.

Gardening has always encouraged my mind to wander. Some of my deeper thoughts have presented themselves while my hands were dirty and three inches deep in soil; granted, not the most perfect time for recording any profound revelations for seasons to come. Still, the messages clearly repeat themselves often enough: learn to wait; learn to have patience. So now I heed the opening of each season's blossoms and in His Own Time, take yet another lesson from my garden.

WHEN I'M REDUCED TO PRAYER

When weakened by dismay, Lord, remind me that You care. Restore in me a thankful heart. Cajole me into prayer! When weakened by life's hurts, Lord, remind me that You live. Restore in me a quiet peace. Teach me to forgive!

When weakened by earth's trials, Lord, remind me that You know. Restore in me a calm repose. Feed me; help me grow! When weakened by life's games, Lord, remind me You are near. Restore in me a sense of trust. Protect me from such fear! When weakened by temptations, Lord, remind me You were man. Restore in me a humble bent. Call me, take my hand!

Summer

We've Each a Place

By what authority proclaimed, by what process or fair measure?

Removing living things deemed irritants…are they not also treasures?

Even seedlings have intrinsic beauty, some small redeeming grace.

Might I not display the buds upon my finest lace?

Dear Lord, who's eye has deemed them such, to reach but never grow?

Should I weed a few, toss them aside, implying that I see

Why I should pull them from the soil – to never fully glow?

And pretend I understand the stewardship You've offered me?

To cast them out from Your green earth, I've found no meaning in this toil.

As gardener I shall choose to find a safe and sandy rest.

Perhaps a place You'd once designed lies hidden in the soil

Let rains renew old garden seeds to proudly sprout their best!

When One Can Only Plant a Thought

How fast my gardener's spade can reap a secret place to pine

Days like these mean petals must oblige: the rules are mine

Know well my heart's disruptive pace, discordant reverie

I'll need no bench; the ground will hold my weakened, soulful me

No need to use a garden hose or soak the planted ground today

My tears will soon enough default 'round stepping stones set deep in clay

The salty drops will wind their way beneath the growth and cut anew

A different path where I might see life's blessings in a different view

Where roses camouflage my wounded mind and frail gait

Mindfully, I enter into His Garden. Let the outside world await!

Stillness comes to comfort who before held anguished fears

When one can only plant a thought…He hears.

Nurturing Garden Blues

Mom would have loved my back yard garden once it had developed after the first few seasons. She would have enjoyed the maturity of the trees and the scattered perennial shrubs. Blue was her favorite color, so the lobelia that I'd dappled here and there to offset the varied pinks and orange hues would have pleased her very much, as it well should since I'd planted it especially with her in mind.

So, too, the Star of Israel blooms that appeared just in time for the Fourth of July every year. It was no coincidence that all of my plants yielded blue flowers. Agapanthus plants, the correct name for the Star of Israel, were indeed survivors; the blossomed "star" bursts of white or blue were used frequently in California as commercial landscaping flora and in highway dividers. They were my kind of plant; nearly indestructible!

I can't tell you how often over the years I had read *"easy to grow"* and believed it! Perhaps it was because Mom could always keep things growing, no matter how delicate the plant; she could revive any greenery in her keeping. She had houseplants that were older than some of her grandchildren! Each plant had a story and held a memory of someone or someplace.

On the other hand, delicate looking vines didn't grow very well under my care. An *"easy to grow"* clematis struggled for its survival and, much to my chagrin, the vine very soon after planting looked like it needed a transfusion. I decided after a few months' efforts that it was really begging for mercy, so I dug it up and disposed of it.

One of my favorite sayings among garden prose is the one that reads,

*One is nearer God's heart in a garden
than anywhere else on earth*

Nurturing an appreciation for flowers and gardens was one of the pleasures Mom and I shared. Refilling our vessels as we did our favorite vases, His grace seemed to quell our anxious souls on many occasions, allowing us just to be. Within the presence of God's mixed bouquets, my mother remains joyfully alongside me.

The Big Porch

When little ones surround us

Or come say hello and share their days,

We can but offer rapt attention!

Habits are from mentors' time-worn ways.

Thank you, Lord! How grateful we are that they climb the walk

To our front door! What? A new feather? A sticker? A toy?

Our porch can hold them all and more!

Every home should have a porch to

Welcome hearts in big and small.

Some banisters to climb on for the ones not yet too tall!

A bit of late day sunshine just to warm a back or two;

A glass of wine and laughter linking grateful hearts to You.

Autumn

When Prayers Waft Through My Garden Bed

A bit of ground had beckoned once; Softened, sandy-colored soil;
Rooted deeply, wherein Choice and Chance diminished symmetry,
Yet offered solace still for me.
Simply, plainly, unadorned…
        Tinted leaves in sky-kissed blue.

When prayers waft through my garden bed,

I find the dreams I'd planted there. A Master's Hand had long ago
        Spread wide the scent-filled plumes,
        So I might seek His Opened Arms.
        Simply, plainly, unadorned…
Rich honey-golden hues.

The Seasons Are But Few

You loaned me once a garden, and whispered quietly,
See what you can create in it with tools and reverie.
You'll draw from each day's tending any lessons meant for you.
Understand the garden beds are loaned; the seasons are but few;
They'll come a time when blossoms fade; remember well their place!
I heard Your admonition as each season showed its face.

I came to know, try after try, each bloom would have one chance
To catch my eye; my stewardship became more joyful with each glance!
Nine years I worked those garden beds; my turn to pass the rake had come.
I one last time watched roses climb; old fashion scents spiced cinnamon.
The lemons, ripened on the tree, awaited the next someone's hand.
Impatiens filled small garden spots, sweet rose-like, ruby, budded strands.

I walked outside the back, recalling once more words You'd said;
I touched the lilies, marguerites; the fuchsias bowed their heads.
Beneath the overhanging branch, I looked up toward the sky.
Releasing hold and heart, I whispered thanks, and accepted why.

od's Country

This was certainly a different place. Here I hadn't level ground for a garden of my own. There were no fences to mark our home's property, just lawns that stretched over what had once been a family farm. We purchased a rolling slope instead, which colored the land with perennial greens of blue and yellowed tints, dusted with a few inches of snow come the winter. Cardinals perched regularly on our deck posts as long as we kept the feeder filled. I soon learned to budget in some wild bird seed each month; were I not faithful, the birds soon found other feeding places in the subdivision and thought twice before returning and giving us a second chance to meet. I had to prove that we transplants were serious if I wanted to enjoy their company!

When the feeder was well filled, chickadees soon joined them; wrens and even blue jays seemed to loiter much longer here than they did among the shrubs we'd had in California. I realized that woodpeckers were tenacious but not necessarily very observant; they could not discern a metal eave from a wooden one! Robins soon discovered our porch and chose our eaves for a nest! Using our front door disturbed them briefly; they would wait until we'd settled down with our glass of wine before they renewed their back and forth trips to the nest.

So you're from California, huh? Whatever brought you here? As though the here were not enough or was remiss in some finer sense... Yes, the area has its troubles and its flaws; but if you want to experience pure, unadulterated patriotism, sport fever, fellowship and sister city festivals, this is the place! Okay, okay; so the humidity is REAL; it is AWFUL; and totally CRUMMY (fill in your adjective)! Yes, there are those days this native Californian could actually believe I understand what it's like to be a goldfish!

You're going to Misery??? I'm not going, you can't make me...

It is your loss, my friend, because you will never see brighter blooms or lovelier seasons or more beautiful cardinals than here in God's country.

Though Frail I Serve Him Still

I can't compare or always stay in step; yet!

He sees my heart, removes the thorn!

He blots dry my tears; His calm quells fears so that I am blind no longer.

You turned away from paths before you; how would you know

From rock or sand? The earth is but happenstance and folly;

Trust in Me, Child... Lend Me your hand!

Serve Him still? Yes, though truly some days I feel frail and worn.

He knows my heart, remembers my name, and

Sees which gifts of mine are the stronger.

Listen! I can hear His whispering;

Go fill the gaps; Turn up the sound! Use your small gifts to

Warm lonely souls. Bring Joy and Peace! Grasp on! Come 'round!

ABOUT THE ARTIST
LEAH JAY

Where color meets imagination, that's where you'll find me!

I'm a self-taught artist and have been exploring various techniques and styles for over 25 years. I left my administrative assistant position four years ago to pursue art full time. Since then I've been able to teach, volunteer, and experiment in just about every type of medium. My dream is to awaken a sense of childlike wonder in as many hearts as possible.

Starting by painting drippy, wet watercolors and acrylics on soaking wet paper – this unpredictable process inspires me, frees my imagination and provides opportunities for "happy accidents" to influence the resulting shapes. Over this vivid foundation, pastel chalks, pencils, pen, and charcoal coax emergent forms from the mass of colors – as traditional subjects like people, characters, and animals, or unplanned abstract adventures. Though I consciously employ both traditional and innovative techniques – my subconscious is the undisputed project manager. In this way I strive to channel pure emotion and energy into my work.

My choice of subjects has included people, celebrities, nature, characters, text-based work, and scenes from fiction and imagination. My art influences include: Sulamith Wulfing, Brian Froud, Alphonse Mucha, Susan Seddon Boulet, and Virgil Finlay. I am inspired by memories of childhood, fairy tales, nature in all its forms, line, color, faces, music, the fantastic and the absurd.

Currently represented by Kaleid Gallery in San Jose, California.

· For more about me: leahjayart.com

ABOUT THE AUTHOR
ANNETTE BROCHIER JOHNSON

Annette is an Oakland, California native and a second-generation American of French descent, the latter was the inspiration for her tongue-in-cheek FrogHavenLady nom de plume! She is the mother of a beautiful daughter with little critters of her own. Writing has been a lifelong passion. Currently, she spends her days at the keyboard in the company of the love of her life Jim at their Frog Haven Home in Washington, Missouri.

Visitors to her FrogHavenLady.com website will find a variety of topics: childhood memories, American legacies, organized religion, politics, motherhood, divorce and remarriage, women in the workplace, and working through personal days of grief, including those from the loss of loved ones by suicide. It is Annette's dry sense of humor, coupled with slightly irreverent viewpoints and ironic commentary on more poignant moments that engage the reader.

For more information, please visit: www.froghavenlady.com

Under Angels' Wings
Epilogue

God provides Earth Angels when we need them most in our lives. Years ago, our daughter had been diagnosed with Juvenile Rheumatoid Arthritis (JRA). She was fourteen years old. A customer of ours submitted her name to his service club; and very soon, we were notified that she had been accepted for treatment by Shriners Hospitals for Children! Until age twenty-one, she was under Shriners loving care.

Like Santa, Earth Angels know where to find us, even when we move two thousand miles from our original stomping grounds. When my Rogue suffered a stroke and later underwent open heart surgery, God's local winged contingent came to our rescue to help us carry a very unfamiliar and daily-changing burden.

During my husband's recovery, God opened another window; I am pursuing my long-wished-for writing profession. My eventual hope is that my writing gifts may serve as yet another conduit, helping fill in the gaps for continued, loving care for little critters in all sizes, like other Shriners Kids.

As He has for us, may God continue to provide earth angels, blessings and new windows of renewed hope and health for you and yours...

aJb

For more information about my Take 5 Donation Program, visit:
www.froghavenlady.com